Learning Short-take®

HIGH PERFORMANCE LEARNING

Creating effective high performance learners

CATHERINE MATTISKE

TPC - The Performance Company Pty Ltd
Level 20, Darling Park
Tower 2, 201 Sussex Street,
Sydney NSW 2000
Australia

ACN 077 455 273
email: tpc@tpc.net.au
Website: www.catherinemattiske.com

© TPC – The Performance Company Pty Limited
First edition published in 2006
Second edition published in 2011
Third edition published in 2022

All rights reserved. Apart from any fair dealing for the purposes of study, research or review, as permitted under Australian copyright law, no part of this publication may be reproduced by any means without the written permission of the copyright owner. Every effort has been made to obtain permission relating to information reproduced in this publication.

The information in this publication is based on the current state of commercial and industry practice, applicable legislation, general law and the general circumstances as at the date of publication. No person shall rely on any of the contents of this publication and the publisher and the author expressly exclude all liability for direct and indirect loss suffered by any person resulting in any way from the use of or reliance on this publication or any part of it. Any options and advice are offered solely in pursuance of the author's and the publisher's intention to provide information, and have not been specifically sought.

For eBook version: By payment of the required fees, you have been granted the non-exclusive, non-transferable right to access and read the text of this e-book on screen. No part of this text may be reproduced, transmitted, downloaded, decompiled, reverse engineered, or stored in or introduced into any information storage retrieval system, in any form or by any means, whether the electronic or mechanical, now known or hereinafter invented, without the express permission of the author.

 A catalogue record for this book is available from the National Library of Australia

National Library of Australia
Cataloguing-in-Publication data

Mattiske, Catherine
High Performance Learning: Creating effective high performance learners

ISBN 978-1-921547-31-7

1. Occupational training 2. Learning I. Title

370.113

Distributed by TPC - The Performance Company - www.catherinemattiske.com
For further information contact TPC - The Performance Company, Sydney Australia on +61 (02) 9555 1953.

HELLO.

Welcome to the Learning Short-take® process!

This Learning Short-take® is a bite sized learning package that aims to improve your skills and provide you with an opportunity for personal and professional development to achieve success in your role.

This Learning Short-take® combines self study with workplace activities in a unique learning system to keep you motivated and energized.
So let's get started!

Step 1:
What's inside?

- Learning Short-take®. This section contains all of the learning content and will guide you through the learning process.
- Learning Activities. You will be prompted to complete these as you read through.
- Learning Journal. This is a summary of your key learnings.
  Update it when prompted.
- Skill Development Action Plan. Learning is about taking action. This is your action plan where you'll plan how you will implement your learning.

Step 2:
Complete the Learning Short-take®

- Learning Short-takes® are best completed in a quiet environment that is free of distractions.
- Schedule time in your calendar to complete the Learning Short-take® and prioritize this time as an investment in your own professional development.
- Depending on the title, most participants complete the Learning Short-take® from 90 minutes to 2.5 hours.

Step 3:
Meet with your Manager/Coach

- Schedule a 30 minute meeting with your Manager or Coach.
- At this meeting share your completed Activities, Learning Journal and Skill Development Action Plan.
- Most importantly, discuss and agree on how you will implement your learning in your role.

GET VIP ACCESS TO YOUR MATERIALS

This Learning Short-take® includes an interactive activity book, associated tools and job aids, plus a bonus eBook.

1 Visit https://www.catherinemattiske.com/books

2 Select your book

3 Click: VIP ACCESS

4 Enter the code: HPL2022177

WELCOME

High Performance Learning
Creating Effective High Performance Learners

High Performance Learning is written for managers and training professionals.

For managers, **High Performance Learning** will assist you in ensuring that your team gets the most out of internal and external training courses and e-learning programs to help meet your personal, team and organizational goals. It provides managers with an understanding of their role in the training process and how they can ensure that team members apply what they have learned after training.

For learning and development professionals, **High Performance Learning** explores strategies to engage managers and key stakeholders with participants throughout the entire learning process – all with minimal effort for you and the manager!

High Performance Learning includes the **Pre-Learning Short-take® Manager Conversation Tool** and the **Post-Learning Short-take® Manager Conversation Tool**, provided as free downloads.

Now let's get started!

1	Learning Short-take® >	Start here
2	Learning Journal	87
3	Skill Development Action Plan	93
4	Quick Reference	99
5	Next Steps	123

> *"I am learning all the time. The tombstone will be my diploma."*
>
> — EARTHA KITT

"

Given Kurzweil's Law of Accelerating Returns, where the speed of evolution increases exponentially, vast societal transformation is likely to occur sooner than anyone expects.

SINGULARITY UNIVERSITY, USA

Section 1

LEARNING SHORT-TAKE®

WHAT'S IN THIS LEARNING SHORT-TAKE®

Table of Contents

How to Complete Your Learning Short-take®	5
Activity Checklist	6
Learning Objectives	7
Let's Get Started	8
Part 1 - The Managers Role in Learning & Development	9
Part 2 - Mattiske's High Performance Learning Model™	15
Part 3 - Providing Support & Influencing Motivation	37
Part 4 - Coaching Learners to High Performance	43
Part 5 - Motivating & Supporting Learners completing Learning Short-takes®	59
Part 6 - Managing Learning Short-takes® - A Step-by-step Guide	73

© 2022, TPC - The Performance Company Pty Limited. All rights reserved.

HOW TO COMPLETE YOUR LEARNING SHORT-TAKE®

1. **Reflect on your skills and abilities** in supporting learners and how you use this information to improve effectiveness in your role.

2. **Complete the Activities as directed.**

3. **Highlight specific skill areas** that you believe you could develop more. Add these to the Learning Journal as you proceed through the Learning Short-take®.

4. When you have completed this Learning Short-take® **meet with your Manager/Coach**. In this meeting, you will jointly establish a personal Skill Development Action Plan.

5. **Subject to your coach's final review** and assessment, you will either sign off the module, or undertake further skill development as appropriate.

"When the student is ready, the master appears."

BUDDHIST PROVERB

Throughout this Learning Short-take® this sign indicates that you should stop and complete an Activity. Do not skip activities and for maximum learning, ensure you complete them as directed.

ACTIVITY CHECKLIST

During this Learning Short-take® you will be prompted to complete the following activities:

- Activity 1 -   Initial Skills Self-Assessment   11
- Activity 2 -   Learning Reflection   22
- Activity 3 -   High Performance Learning Model™ Match   30
- Activity 4 -   High Performance Learning Model™ - Team Mapping   34
- Activity 5 -   High Performance Learning Model™ - Manager Influence   42
- Activity 6 -   Coaching Opportunity - High Performance Learner   47
- Activity 7 -   Coaching Opportunity - Independent Learner   51
- Activity 8 -   Coaching Opportunity - Abandoned and/or Passive Learner   57
- Pre-Learning Short-take® Manager Conversation Tool   80
- Post-Learning Short-take® Manager Conversation Tool   86
- Learning Journal   87
- Skill Development Action Plan   93

LEARNING OBJECTIVES

By the end of this Learning Short-take® you should be able to:

- Analyze a self-assessment regarding Manager involvement before, during and after employees' learning and development
- Define each element of Mattiske's High Performance Learning Model™
- Complete a High Performance Learning Model™ matrix for a case study and actual scenario
- Coach employees throughout the learning process with the aim of creating high performance
- Use TPC tools to assist in before and after learning conversations
- Create a Skill Development Action Plan.

"I don't think much of a man who is not wiser today than he was yesterday."

ABRAHAM LINCOLN

LET'S GET STARTED

Deciding on appropriate training and development for an individual or an entire team is a skill in itself, however few Managers are formally taught this process. Once the decision has been made the Manager plays a vital role in supporting and motivating employees throughout the entire process of learning and development. How a Manager sets up the training, talks to employees before the learning, then how they work with the employee after the learning plays an important role in the amount of learning the employee transfers to their job.

This Learning Short-take® will support Managers to assist individuals and teams when embarking on professional development. You will learn how critical the Managers' role is before, during and after employees attend training, or engage in any other method of learning. The Learning Short-take® uses a number of case studies as well as opportunity to explore real life management challenges and opportunities.

> While the focus of this Learning Short-take® is for managers, professional trainers will gain insight into how to engage managers and participants throughout the learning process.

THE PIVOTAL ROLE IN TRAINING: THE MANAGER

When it comes to employee learning and development, Managers play a critical role before, during and after the learning. Managers don't have to be trainers. Right now, you are completing a Learning Short-take® and throughout this program Learning Short-takes® are used as the example of employee learning program.

For instructor-led training, e-learning, virtual, or distance learning, or any other type of training, the process is similar: the Manager sets the stage for learning to begin, ensures that the employee attends the training and follows up after the training.

All training requires a return on investment by way of an improvement in employee skills and or knowledge. This improvement is generally referred to in the corporate training profession as **'a change in behavior'**. It should be the expectation of all Managers that after participants have attended any type of training or have completed a module of learning (such as a Learning Short-take®) that **'something will be done differently as a result'**. **'Something different'** means that a change of behavior has taken place.

How involved a Manager is in the learning process could be the difference for the company's return on its training investment. TPC refers to Learning Short-takes® as a type of **Partnership Learning**. For other types of training, Partnership Learning may also apply. **Partnership Learning means that the Manager partners with his or her employee before, during, and after the learning to maximize the change of behavior.**

 **Complete Activity # 1**
Initial Skills Self-Assessment

ACTIVITY 1: INITIAL SKILLS SELF-ASSESSMENT

Understanding how you currently manage your people throughout their learning and development is a good starting point to identify your strengths and areas for development. This assessment covers the key skills required to maximize high performance learners, in order to improve learning outcomes and job success.

Step 1 - Rate yourself on each of the techniques.
7 is competent and confident, little need for improvement
4 is average, needs improvement
1 is uncomfortable, major need for improvement

Step 2 - Note specific areas of improvement related to each that you would like to develop. Be sure to include your reasons for your rating in each skill, as this reasoning will be a key part of the initial goal setting session which follows.

Step 3 - Begin thinking about a personal development plan and identify 2 or 3 things you could do to improve your skills in this area and write them in the space provided.

I…	Rating	Reasoning
believe in the necessity and value of developing myself professionally	1 2 3 4 5 6 7	
believe in the necessity and value of developing my team professionally	1 2 3 4 5 6 7	
work with each member of my team on a regular basis to develop an individual development plan	1 2 3 4 5 6 7	
actively listen to when my team talks about training that they need	1 2 3 4 5 6 7	
discuss learning opportunities at performance review time	1 2 3 4 5 6 7	
discuss learning opportunities at times other than performance review time	1 2 3 4 5 6 7	
know the competency framework of my organization or use one of my own	1 2 3 4 5 6 7	
know who is at training, and who is completing other types of learning	1 2 3 4 5 6 7	
talk to each member of my team prior to them attending a training course	1 2 3 4 5 6 7	

(continued)

ACTIVITY 1: CONTINUED

I...	Rating	Reasoning
discuss the course objectives with those attending training and list what their expectations are according to their job role	1 2 3 4 5 6 7	
talk to each member of my team prior to them completing e-learning, virtual, or distance learning or any other non-instructor-led program	1 2 3 4 5 6 7	
verbally support organizational learning initiatives, regardless of how they impact me personally	1 2 3 4 5 6 7	
monitor the motivation levels of each of my team when they are registered for a training program	1 2 3 4 5 6 7	
have methods and processes to support individuals and my team before, during and after their learning	1 2 3 4 5 6 7	
have established rewards for learning and development	1 2 3 4 5 6 7	
lead by example, by attending relevant training, conferences and display an interest in my **own** learning to the benefit of the organization	1 2 3 4 5 6 7	
offer choices to individuals and the entire team about their professional development	1 2 3 4 5 6 7	
provide a secure learning environment – one in which its okay to fail while learning or practicing a new skill	1 2 3 4 5 6 7	
provide time to learn and practice new skills after a formal training course	1 2 3 4 5 6 7	

Personal development plan ideas:

1

2

Now update your Learning Journal (page 87)

MATCHING SKILLS TO ORGANIZATIONAL PRIORITIES

Deciding on appropriate training for an individual or an entire team is a skill in itself, however few Managers are formally taught this process. Most Managers are left to determine the training needs for their team, based on their best judgment and what information comes across their desk about training. Some Managers work closely with their HR department or Training department to help determine their training needs giving them the benefit of professional advice.

Often an organization has an automated competency mapping process, linked to their performance review system, which helps Managers match organizational competencies to an individual's current skill set. However, many organizations leave it to individual Managers to work out the development needs for each member of their team.

In order to do this, a Manager should be aware of each individual's strengths and weaknesses, as well as those of the team as a whole. With this information, the Manager cross-references the current skills with the needs of the organization and has a clear road map of what projects are on the horizon for the team. By doing this, the Manager may quickly decide what learning programs are valuable and which are unnecessary for the team to pursue.

BEING PROACTIVE ABOUT LEARNING

Effective Managers encourage a culture of learning and development and should suggest training to employees.

Rather than wait for an employee to request training, or wait for performance review time, a Manager should be proactive and study the business needs and employees skills to decide who needs training in which areas.

"Anyone who stops learning is old, whether at twenty or eighty"

HENRY FORD

Now update your Learning Journal (page 87)

MATTISKE'S HIGH PERFORMANCE LEARNING MODEL™

PART 2

INTRODUCING MATTISKE'S HIGH PERFORMANCE LEARNING MODEL™

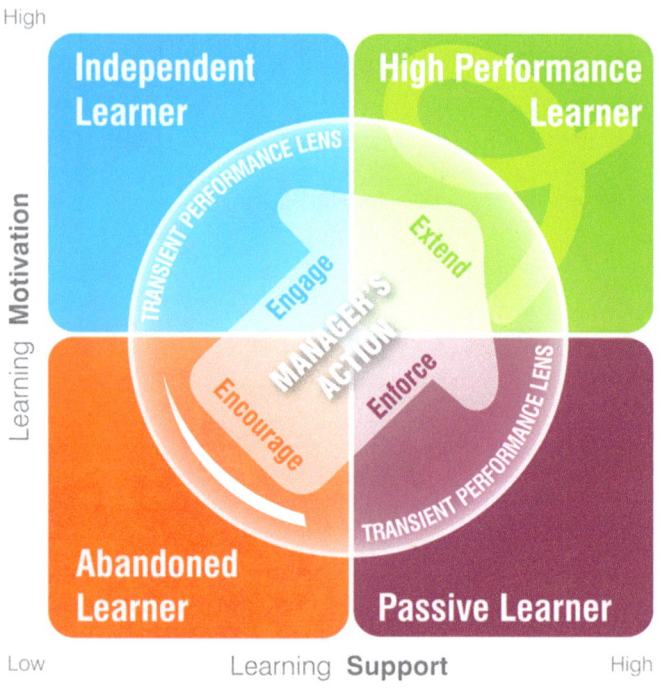

Mattiske's High Performance Learning Model (2006) was developed as a visual representation of the role of the Manager and trainer and how they impact participant success in corporate training.

The Paradox of Leadership

The paradox of today's organization is that Managers and Leaders strive to achieve their vision and organizational objectives and most believe that training and development of their people is integral, yet, some do little to actively support the learning process and application of learning.

Learning cynicism in action

Most Managers verbally support the learning and development of their employees. However, often a Manager's actions speak louder than words.

Often Managers send their employee to training courses without setting any expectations. After returning from the training course Managers may hurriedly ask follow-up questions as they pass the employee in the hallway, such as 'how was the training course?' to which the employee says "fine"; "fine" says the Manager, and both Manager and employee keep walking! This rushed scenario (while it may be a dramatization) gives permission to the employee to have little to no accountability to apply what they have learned into their day-to-day work.

In the training profession this approach is often cynically referred to as the 'spray and pray' approach to training - where employees are 'sprayed' with new information and skills and Managers 'pray' that it sticks!

"Man's mind, once stretched by a new idea, never regains its original dimensions."

OLIVER WENDELL HOLMES

HIGH PERFORMANCE LEARNING MODEL™ IN DETAIL

High Performance Learning Model™ in action

Mattiske's High Performance Learning Model™ clearly places accountability for the success of learning with both the Manager and the employee by forming a shared responsibility for the learning success therefore **Manager and employee partner for success.**

Each Learning Short-take® developed by The Performance Company puts the latest adult learning research into action and links directly to the breakthrough concept of Partnership Learning.

Mattiske's High Performance Learning Model™ describes four types of learners:
The High Performance Learner, The Independent Learner, The Abandoned Learner **and** The Passive Learner.

The aim of Mattiske's High Performance Learning Model™ is to help Managers and trainers **increase the number of naturally occurring High Performance Learners** by providing high Learning Support and encouraging high Learning Motivation.

The center arrow, pointing to the High Performance Learner provides the ways for Managers to assist their employees to become High Performance Learners.

THE FOUR LEARNER TYPES

- **The High Performance Learner**
- **The Independent Learner**
- **The Abandoned Learner**
- **The Passive Learner**

The four Learner Types are not designed to 'box' people into one type or another. One employee may be simultaneously all four Learner Types, or just one, two, or three.

Transient Performance Lens

One person may transition from one Learner Type to another depending on the learning that they are about to encounter, or the learning they are participating in at the time.

They may even transition *during* a training program, entering the training program as one Learner Type, and then changing midstream (either positively or negatively) depending on what's happening during the training.

Examples of 'The Transient Learner'

The following examples show how two individuals approach learning. It shows two different learners attending role specific programs that include two of the same programs (Customer Service, and Occupational Health and Safety). The following case studies show how different the outcomes can be.

Example 1:
Chris - The Accountant

Chris' Personal High Performance Learning Model™

Chris an Accountant is a **High Performance Learner** on a new program regarding **Triple Bottom Line Accounting** - a topic about which his Manager is passionate.

The same accountant, Chris, is an **Independent Learner** in an external **Master of Business Administration (MBA) program,**

an **Abandoned Learner** in the new **Customer Service program** and

a **Passive Learner** when registered onto a new company wide **Occupational Health and Safety program.**

Example 2:
Peter - The Customer Service Representative

(Peter's Personal High Performance Learning Model™)

In another example, Peter a customer service representative, is a **High Performance Learner** on the new **customer service program,**

an **Independent Learner** during a **Telephone Skills program,**

an **Abandoned Learner** in the new **Occupational Health and Safety program** and

a **Passive Learner** during a training course on **Customer Accounting 101.**

Complete Activity # 2
Learning Reflection

ACTIVITY 2: LEARNING REFLECTION

1 - List different formal and informal learning programs that **you** have completed over recent time. (Include training courses, conferences, short-courses, higher education, technical certification, self study, books purchased for the purpose of learning new skills, e-learning, virtual learning, or other distance learning, etc)

Learning Program Name	2	3

2 - Reflect on your own level of motivation. In Column 2 write the heading **Motivation**. For each learning program you completed reflect on your level of personal motivation **before, during and after** the learning. In Column 2 - For each program write **H** when you have felt high motivation, or **L** when you have felt low motivation in relation to the program.

3 - Reflect on the level of support you received from your Manager. In Column 3 write the heading **Support**. For each learning program you completed reflect on the level of support you received **before, during and after** the learning. In Column 3 - Write **H** for high support, or **L** for low support for each program.

ACTIVITY 2: CONTINUED

4 - Using Mattiske's High Performance Learning Model™ below, map your Personal High Performance Learning Model™. Plot each of the learning programs in their respective Learner Types.

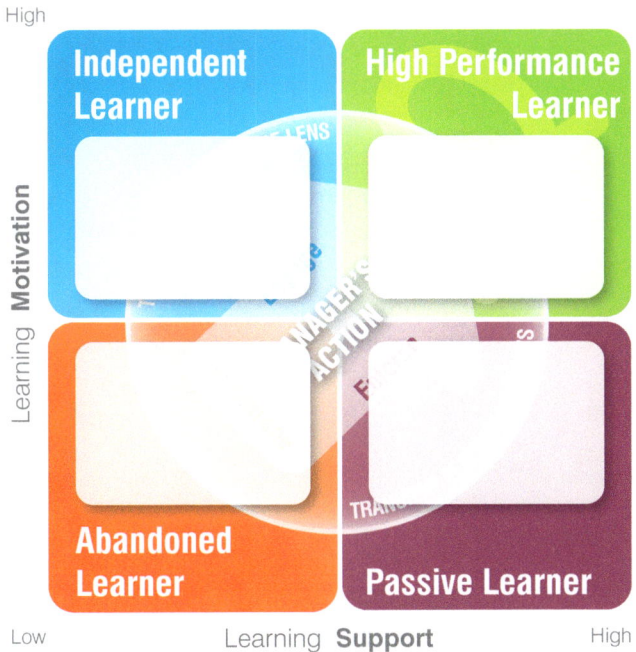

5 - Reflect on the result of your Personal High Performance Learning Model™. How does this result link to your role as a Manager, as you manage others in their learning?

_____
_____
_____

Now update your Learning Journal (page 87)

THE FOUR LEARNER TYPES EXPLAINED

The High Performance Learner

High Motivation (Intrinsic) + High Support (Extrinsic)

The High Performance Learner typically enjoys learning. They have an internal drive for changing their behavior and are adaptable to change, viewing it as a learning opportunity. They may initiate projects to implement learning and see the learning benefit as much about the organization as themselves. They will most likely teach others and willingly share their learning. They are self-motivated and want to show the results of implementing learning.

Before the Learning

Before a training session, or learning intervention, they ensure that they have completed pre-requisites, know where and when the learning is to take place, scheduled their workload to accommodate their learning, made personal arrangements to ensure that their focus is on the learning, and potentially begun the learning process by undertaking reading or research prior to the formal learning. They will have been briefed by their Manager or received some communication regarding the value of the upcoming learning and will have been provided with details about the course - a course outline, overview, etc.

During the Learning

They are an active learner during training, usually taking notes and asking questions to clarify and extend their learning. They find opportunities to learn in both formal and informal settings. Learning is their focus, rather than it being a directive from the organization. During the learning, they are thinking of ways of how they will apply their learning and have a 'can't wait to get back to work and apply it' attitude.

Distinctively during the learning, if they don't understand an element of what they are being taught, they don't get stuck, they either ask for clarification immediately or take note of the question and should it not be addressed further in the program ask it later.

After the Learning

They are quick to implement their learning and are usually eager to report their progress to their Manager. If Managers do solicit feedback, the employee provides a detailed account of the program and generally offer information on how they will apply their learning without extensive manager prompting. They will teach others and willingly share their learning. Informal learning may continue as they self discover more advanced and in-depth content.

The Independent Learner

High Motivation (Intrinsic) + High Support (Extrinsic)

The Independent Learner has many positive traits due to their high motivation for learning. Like the High Performance Learner they are active and keen learners with high participation before, during and after the learning intervention. They are self-motivated, quick to research learning opportunities, and use their work time to learn and enhance their skills.

However, the Independent Learner has little support from their organization. This lack of support may present itself in several ways: the learner may initiate the learning which may be offered internally or externally to the organization, their Manager may have said negative things about the upcoming learning program yet despite this the Independent Learner attends and applies the learning. They may increase their skills and knowledge completely by their own self direction without the need for any formal training course or cost outlay by their organization.

The Independent Learner is often a high achiever, climbing the corporate ladder in a very visible way due to their own commitment to self-development.

Organizational Risk

The Independent Learner may also be a risk to the organization. Due to lack of organizational support, they are not being rewarded for their self-development and in-turn may not be a long-term employee, becoming  disengaged with the organization. they are likely not to share their knowledge with their co-workers and over time may disengage from their team.

But...we paid for the training!

Financial support for external study is often not seen as support for learning at all, but more of a way of achieving self-development with company funding as a way of promoting the individual or preparing them to leave the company with their new qualifications in hand. In this case, the Independent Leaner will be keen to push their environment by influencing their Manager to approve the purchase of books, materials, external courses, internal courses, off-site educational opportunities, conferences, and formal higher education.

How do I know if I have an Independent Learner

The Independent Learner often comes to their performance review meeting with their well-researched learning plan in hand ready to discuss. They will ensure that their individual development plan is well documented in their performance review, and will ensure that they complete or exceed it.

The Independent Learner often spends their work time completing external course assignments, utilizing company equipment, time and resources for private use. Learning is generally about them, not how their learning will help the organization in the long term.

The Abandoned Learner

High Motivation (Intrinsic) + High Support (Extrinsic)

The Abandoned Learner has low Learning Motivation and low Learning Support, resulting in little or no behavior change as a result of the learning program.

Abandoned Learners attend training and may participate just enough to complete the program. Their motivation extends only to "get through the training". Before the training they may complete their prerequisites to ensure that they remain out of the trainer's spotlight, or not. Abandoned Learners often have sophisticated yet fabricated reasons for not completing pre-course work, arriving late, having to leave early, and if challenged, they may have sophisticated reasons why they have not implemented what they have learned.

The Abandoned Learners' manager and organization is doing little to provide support and encouragement for their learning further supporting their lack of motivation.

If asked by their Manager 'how was the training?" they are likely to respond in a one word or short answer, to which their Manager may say 'good', and that's the limit of the conversation.

Quite simply, Abandoned Learners are unmotivated and their Manager doesn't care!

The Passive Learner

Low Motivation (Intrinsic) + High Support (Extrinsic)

The Passive Learner is like the Abandoned Learner both sharing a lack of motivation. The difference between the two is the amount of support provided by their Manager and organization.

Passive learners have high support for implementing their learning yet choose not to change their behavior. Passive learners attend the training program, and like Abandoned Learners do what is needed to 'get through'.

Support may be given in a formal and non-formal ways. Formal support may be by way of systems and technology provided by the organization to test-drive new skills, refresher training, formal coaching sessions with mentors, coaches, peers or Managers. Informal support may be Manager guidance and coaching, peer-to-peer feedback sessions, and buddy systems. **The Passive Learner has a variety of formal and non-formal support mechanisms in place, has attended the learning program, yet still hasn't implemented what has been learned and has not changed their behavior.**

Passive learners may think that the new company direction is 'flavor of the month' and 'if they just ignore it, it will pass by'. In short, being a Passive Learner is not a training issue; Passive Learners have a performance issue. Everything has been provided by the organization to set up a successful learning transition and outcome, yet the employee isn't changing their behavior.

Complete Activities 3 & 4
High Performance Learning Model™ Match / Team Mapping

ACTIVITY 3: HIGH PERFORMANCE LEARNING MODEL™ MATCH

Match the Learner Type with their characteristics. There may be more than one Learner Type for each of the statements. Put a X in the Learner Type that displays the characteristic. There may be up to two correct answers per statement.

	High Performance Learner	Independent Learner	Abandoned Learner	Passive Learner
Before a training session, or learning intervention, they ensure that they have completed pre-requisites.				
Due to the lack of support, they are likely not to share their knowledge with their co-workers and over time may disengage from their team.				
During the learning, they are taking note of how they will apply their learning and have a 'can't wait to get back to work and apply it' attitude.				
Everything has been provided by the organization to set up a successful learning transition and outcome, yet the employee isn't changing their behavior.				
There is little or no behavior change as a result of the learning program and they do what they need 'to get through the program'.				
They are active and keen learners with high participation before, during and after the learning intervention.				
They are quick to implement their learning and are usually eager to report their progress to their Manager.				
They are self-motivated and want to show the results of implementing learning.				

ACTIVITY 3: CONTINUED

	High Performance Learner	Independent Learner	Abandoned Learner	Passive Learner
They are unmotivated and their Manager doesn't care.				
They have sophisticated yet fabricated reasons for not completing pre-course work, arriving late, having to leave early, and if challenged by their Manager, they may have sophisticated reasons why they have not implemented what they have learned.				
They may initiate projects to implement learning and see the learning benefit as much about the organization as themselves.				
They often come to their performance review meeting with their well-researched learning plan in hand ready to discuss which will likely include non-job related learning programs.				
They often spend their work time completing external course assignments, utilizing company equipment, time and resources for private use. Learning is about them, not how their learning will help the organization in the long term.				
They will be keen to push their environment by influencing their Manager to approve the purchase of books, materials, external courses, internal courses, off-site educational opportunities and formal higher education.				

ACTIVITY 3: CHECK YOUR ANSWERS

Check your answers to the previous activity. If you have made an error, go back to the description of each Learner Type to ensure you are clear on characteristic.

	High Performance Learner	Independent Learner	Abandoned Learner	Passive Learner
Before a training session, or learning intervention, they ensure that they have completed pre-requisites.	X	X		
Due to the lack of support, they are likely not to share their knowledge with their co-workers and over time may disengage from their team.		X		
During the learning, they are taking note of how they will apply their learning and have a 'can't wait to get back to work and apply it' attitude.	X			
Everything has been provided by the organization to set up a successful learning transition and outcome, yet the employee isn't changing their behavior.				X
There is little or no behavior change as a result of the learning program and they do what they need 'to get through the program'.			X	X
They are active and keen learners with high participation before, during and after the learning intervention.	X	X		
They are quick to implement their learning and are usually eager to report their progress to their Manager.	X			
They are self-motivated and want to show the results of implementing learning.	X			

ACTIVITY 3: CHECK YOUR ANSWERS

	High Performance Learner	Independent Learner	Abandoned Learner	Passive Learner
They are unmotivated and their Manager doesn't care.			X	
They have sophisticated yet fabricated reasons for not completing pre-course work, arriving late, having to leave early, and if challenged by their Manager, they may have sophisticated reasons why they have not implemented what they have learned.			X	X
They may initiate projects to implement learning and see the learning benefit as much about the organization as themselves.	X			
They often come to their performance review meeting with their well-researched learning plan in hand ready to discuss which will likely include non-job related learning programs.		X		
They often spend their work time completing external course assignments, utilizing company equipment, time and resources for private use. Learning is about them, not how their learning will help the organization in the long term.		X		
They will be keen to push their environment by influencing their Manager to approve the purchase of books, materials, external courses, internal courses, off-site educational opportunities and formal higher education.		X		

Now update your Learning Journal (page 87)

ACTIVITY 4: HIGH PERFORMANCE LEARNING MODEL™ - TEAM MAPPING

1 - List below learning programs that your **whole team** has completed in recent times. (If your entire team hasn't completed any one program together, then list each team members name with a program that they have completed individually)

_____

_____

_____

_____

_____

2 - Using Mattiske's High Performance Learning Model™ on the following page, map the High Performance Learning Model™ for your entire team Plot each of the learning programs in their respective Learner Types. (You may wish to choose one program, or plot all programs). On each of the Learning Type quadrants write employee names. This activity is based entirely on your perception of the level of support that you and the organization provided, and your perception of each individual's level of motivation. There is no ideal answer, only a visual representation of your perception. (If you have listed separate programs for each team member write their name and the program name in the quadrant.)

Example:

Negotiating Skills - Completed Team Map

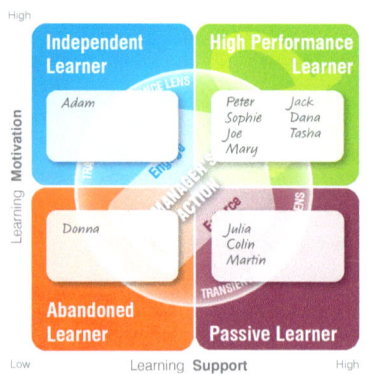

ACTIVITY 4: CONTINUED

Learning Program Name: _____

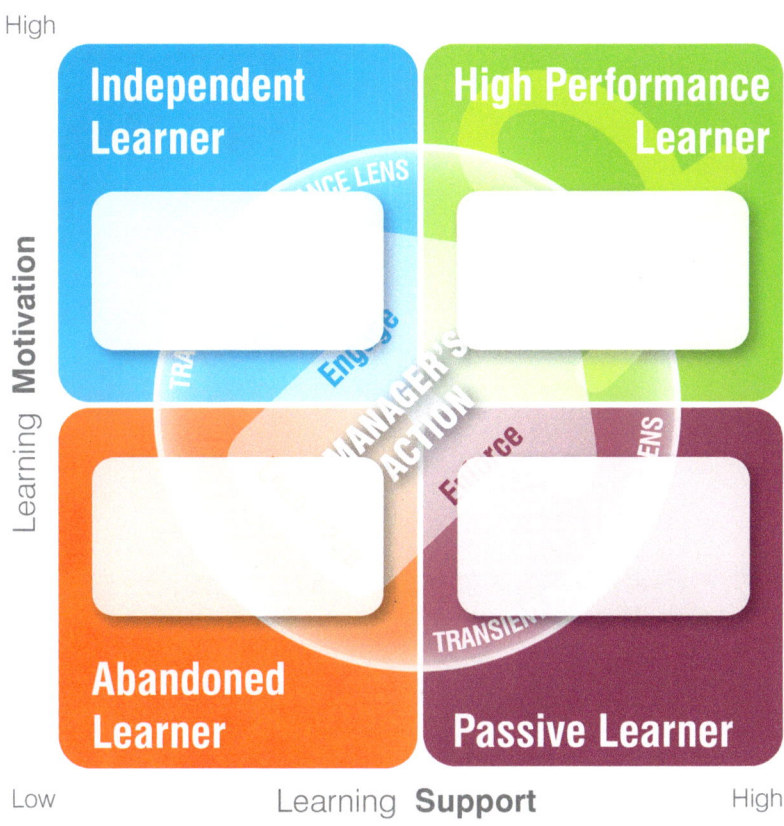

ACTIVITY 4: CONTINUED

3 - Reflect on the result of the Team Map on Mattiske's High Performance Learning Model™. How does this result link to your role as a Manager, as you manage others in their learning?

_____
_____
_____
_____
_____
_____
_____
_____
_____
_____
_____
_____
_____

Now update your Learning Journal (page 87)

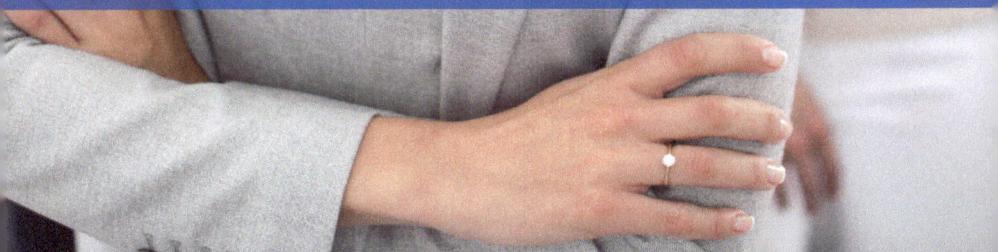

PROVIDING SUPPORT & INFLUENCING MOTIVATION

PART 3

SUPPORTING LEARNING & INFLUENCING MOTIVATION

Managers positively influence the employee's external environment by providing high levels of Learning Support. Managers may also have a negative influence on learning, often by doing or saying seemingly minor things or with offhand, jokey or flippant remarks.

Example 1: Chris - The Accountant - Manager's Influence

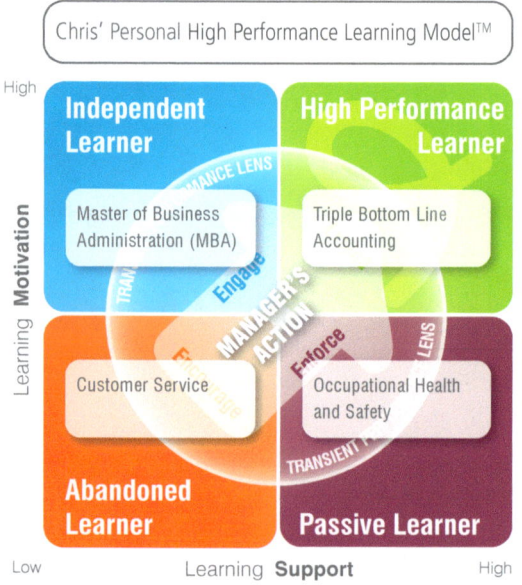

Using the example in the previous section, it is useful to explore how Chris' Manager may have inadvertently influenced Chris towards the learning outcome of the four programs Chris attended.

- Chris' Manager is passionate about **Triple Bottom Line Accounting** and discussed at length the advantages of learning this with Chris and offered to personally coach Chris if needed **(High Learning Support)**. Chris was excited about going to the training course **(High Learning Motivation)**.

- Chris is enthusiastic and driven to complete his **MBA** (**High Learning Motivation**) and the company pays the university fees, however his Manager never mentions Chris' progress outside of his performance review at which time Chris presents his Manager with the invoice for the next round of classes (**Low Learning Support**).

- Chris' Manager said in a team meeting that "we all have to do this ridiculous **Customer Service** training" which sent a very clear message that it wasn't for non-client-facing employees, which included Chris (**Low Learning Support**). Chris attended the training because he had to (**Low Learning Motivation**).

- On the day before the final deadline for completion, Chris finished a very high-tech e-learning session on **Occupational Health and Safety** and completed the final on-line assessment (after two attempts). Chris' Manager is very keen on ensuring his team meets the new corporate standards. Chris is yet to read the accompanying handbook, complete the post-session task and hasn't implemented anything from the program in which Chris' organization has invested heavily (**High Learning Support, Low Learning Motivation**).

Example 2: Peter - The Customer Service Representative - Manager's Influence

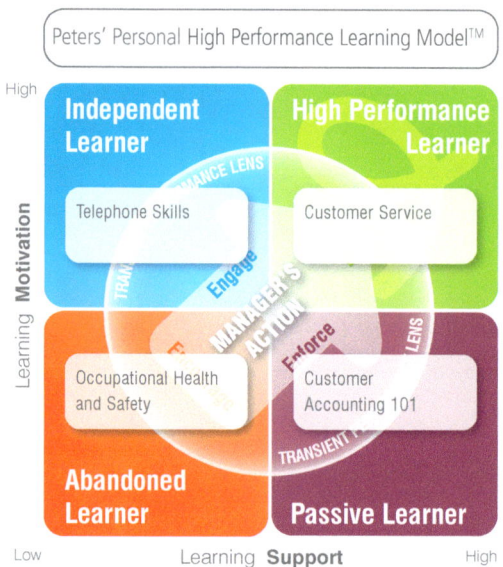

Using the example in the previous section, it is useful to explore how Peter's Manager may have intentionally and inadvertently influenced Peter.

- Peter is a young Manager climbing the corporate ladder. His passion is customer service and hopes to manage the customer service department in the future. Peter's Manager met with the entire customer service team and provided program expectations and how the program links directly to the customer service representative role. After the training, Peter continued to be a High Performance Learner in **Customer Service** and now provides 'buddy' support to others in his team.
- Peter approached his Manager during performance review time about an internal training program on **Telephone Skills**. His Manager agreed that Peter could attend the program. Since attending, Peter's Manager hasn't talked about it at all. Peter learned lots of great things in the program

which he uses on a daily basis, however in Peter's opinion his manager isn't interested in what he has learned. Also, he's sure his team could benefit from same of these new learning however he hasn't been given the chance to share that learning.

- Peter was registered to complete the e-learning program for **Occupational Health and Safety**. His Manager sent an email to say 'get it done by Friday'. Peter had to complete the program in between telephone calls. The e-learning program started with a pre-assessment. Peter guessed the answers and to his amazement got 65% correct which meant that he could whiz through the rest of the module. He completed the e-learnings by skim reading each section and guessing the answers. Peter was given credit in the Learning Management System for completion of the module. Peter's Manager hasn't mentioned it since. Peter did not implement anything from the module.
- Peter has struggled with mathematics all through his schooling. Peter received notification from the training department that all customer service representatives were required to complete a two-day **Customer Accounting 101**. Peter apprehensively attended the course, however had 'accidentally' booked a doctor's appointment at 2pm on the first day which meant he missed 25% of the program. The company invested heavily in entry level accounting for all staff, however Peter has no interest. He nervously awaits a team meeting next week, where he knows a progress check for the program is on the agenda.

Complete Activity 5
High Performance Learning Model™ - Manager Influence

ACTIVITY 5: HIGH PERFORMANCE LEARNING MODEL™ - MANAGER INFLUENCE

1. Review the previous activity where you created your Team High Performance Learning Model™.

2. Contemplate your actions as a Manager. What influence did you have on your team, either intentionally or inadvertently that may have influenced the outcome of their learning?

3. Choose one person from each Learning Type and complete the table below.

	High Performance Learner	Independent Learner	Abandoned Learner	Passive Learner
Name of team member that is in this quadrant (refer to Team Map on Mattiske's High Performance Learning Model™).				
What positive things have you done or said (intentionally or inadvertently) that may have influenced this person's learning outcome.				
What negative things have you done or said (intentionally or inadvertently) that may have influenced this person's learning outcome.				

Now update your Learning Journal (page 87)

COACHING LEARNERS TO HIGH PERFORMANCE

PART 4

COACHING 4 LEARNER TYPES TO HIGH PERFORMANCE LEARNERS

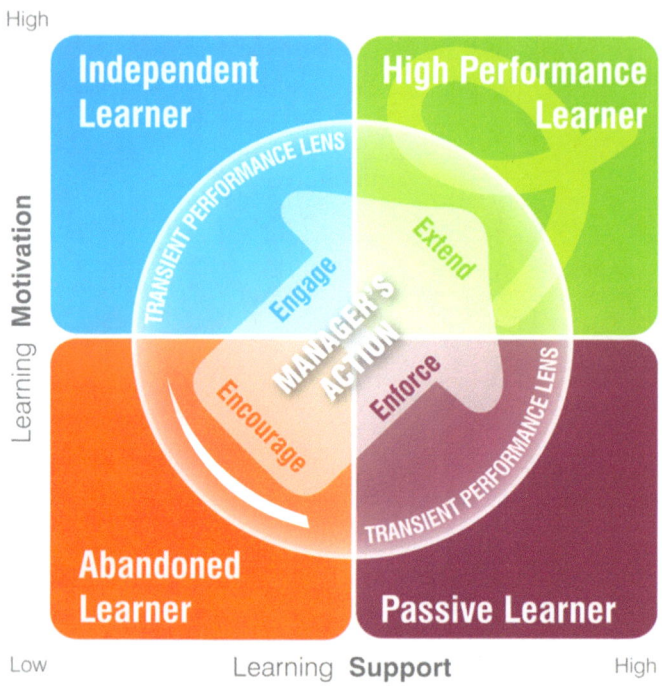

Using Mattiske's High Performance Learning Model™, we now focus on the arrow in the center of the model. **The aim of the Manager is to coach all employees to become High Performance Learners.**

There is no fail proof solution - rather a collection of ideas that Managers may use to influence participant motivation and provide learning support.

For team members who already display the Learning Type of **High Performance Learner** it's important that the Manager continue to coach them to maintain their **High Performance Learner** status.

MAXIMIZING HIGH PERFORMANCE LEARNERS - EXTEND

The **High Performance Learner** already displays high levels of motivation towards learning. Also, the already apparent high levels of learning support fuel them to even greater learning achievement.

They have applied their learning on the job and are comfortable in their ability to do it well. **High Performance Learners** may be coaching others in the team formally or informally. Due to their high level of motivation, they may explore more in-depth knowledge of the subject autonomously.

The goal for Managers is to Extend High Performance Learners to achieve higher levels of performance.

Ideas for Managing High Performance Learners

- **Reward High Performance Learners on their achievement.** Rewards may be as simple as a private conversation or highlighting their uptake of new skills to the rest of the team in a team meeting, or a tangible reward, if appropriate. Publicly rewarding the High Performance Learner is an effective reward for them and also displays the Manager's commitment to implementing learning to the other members of the team.

- **Agree on learning goals.** Discuss their Skill Development Action Plan. Ensure that each part of the learning program has a relevant action item. Ensure that each action item links to their role and their current and future projects.

- **Monitor their progress** towards successful implementation of their Skill Development Action Plan. Ensure that barriers that may get in their way of achieving their learning goals are removed.

- **Stretch learning goals.** Where appropriate discuss ways of stretching their Skill Development Action Plan to further advancement. Perhaps partner them with an Abandoned or Passive Learner having them provide a 'buddy coaching role'. This form of co-operative learning may extend the High Performance Learner and may also encourage their co-worker to increase their motivation for learning.

- **Discuss Support Mechanisms.** Talk about what support is in place for them and how they may access the support.

- **Review Progress and Provide Feedback.** Ensure that regular meetings are scheduled to check in on their progress. Continuously provide encouragement.

Complete Activity # 6
Coaching Opportunity - High Performance Learner

ACTIVITY 6: COACHING OPPORTUNITY - HIGH PERFORMANCE LEARNER

1. Review the previous activity where you created your **Team High Performance Learning Model™**.
2. **Choose one person** who you consider a High Performance Learner.
3. **Schedule a meeting with this person.**
4. Use the form below to **plan your conversation** with the employee.

Employee Name:		**Program:**
Ideas for Managing High Performance Learners	**Pre-meeting preparation**	**Notes**
Reward High Performance Learners on their achievement. Rewards may be as simple as a private conversation or highlighting their uptake of new skills to the rest of the team in a team meeting, or a tangible reward, if appropriate.	How will you reward this person on their High Performance regarding the learning that they have just undertaken?	
Agree on learning goals. Discuss their Skill Development Action Plan. Ensure that each part of the learning program has a relevant action item. Ensure that each action item links to their role and their current and future projects.	Print a copy of their job description and keep it on hand ready for the meeting. How does their job role link to the learning that they have just undertaken?	
Monitor their progress towards successful implementation of their Skill Development Action Plan. Ensure that barriers that may get in their way of achieving their learning goals are removed.	What barriers would you predict may get in their way to completing their Skill Development Action Plan? (You'll discover more at the meeting, however some pre-thinking will send a strong message that you are supporting their development).	

ACTIVITY 6: CONTINUED

Ideas for Managing High Performance Learners	Pre-meeting preparation	Notes
Stretch learning goals. Where appropriate discuss ways of stretching their Skill Development Action Plan to further advancement. Perhaps partner them with an Abandoned or Passive Learner having them provide a 'buddy coaching role'. This form of co-operative learning may extend the High Performance Learner and may also encourage their co-worker to increase their motivation for learning.	What ideas do you have for them to stretch their goals? (You'll discover more at the meeting, however some pre-thinking will send a strong message that you are supporting their development).	
Discuss Support Mechanisms. Talk about what support is in place for them and how they may access the support.	What support mechanisms are already in place?	
	What support mechanisms can you put in place for them?	
	Who else can support them?	
Review Progress and Provide Feedback. Ensure that regular meetings are scheduled to check in on their progress. Continuously provide encouragement.	What is the very next step to follow-up progress?	
	When should you schedule the next meeting?	

Now update your Learning Journal (page 87)

MANAGING INDEPENDENT LEARNERS - ENGAGE

The **Independent Learner** displays high levels of motivation, however requires Manager Learning Support in order to become a **High Performance Learner.**

Learners may have applied their learning on the job and are comfortable in their ability to do it well, however have probably not shared their learning with others.

If they have not applied their learning on the job, they may have completed the learning for their own personal benefit. In this regard, they have little or no intention of using their learning in their current role, and may have attended the learning for future roles within their current organization or with a new organization.

The goal for Managers is to Engage Independent Learners, that is coach them to share their learning and be *a part of the team* to achieve higher levels of performance.

Ideas for Managing Independent Learners

- **Discuss the learning program.** Meet with the team member to discuss what happened during the learning program. Talk about what they learned, and most importantly how their learning links to their current role. Acknowledge completion of the learning and reward their achievement appropriately.

- **Agree on learning goals.** If they have developed a Skill Development Action Plan discuss the actions that they have listed. Ensure that the actions listed are relevant to their current role. If they have not developed a Skill Development Action Plan, work side-by-side with them to create it. Working together on this will send a strong message of support to the learner.
- **Monitor their progress** towards goal achievement. Ensure that barriers that may get in their way of achieving their learning goals are removed.
- **Stretch learning goals.** Where appropriate discuss ways of bringing the employee into the team. Perhaps partner them with an Abandoned or Passive Learner having them provide a 'buddy coaching role'. Alternatively, they could work on developing new workplans, procedures or policies by partnering with a High Performance Learner. This form of co-operative learning may extend the Independent Learner and may encourage their lower performing peers to increase their motivation for learning.
- **Discuss Support Mechanisms.** Talk about what support is in place for the employee and how they may access the support.
- **Review Progress and Provide Feedback.** Ensure that regular meetings are scheduled to check in on their progress. Continuously provide encouragement.

Complete Activity # 7
Coaching Opportunity - Independent Learner

ACTIVITY 7: COACHING OPPORTUNITY - INDEPENDENT LEARNER

1. Review the previous activity where you created your **Team High Performance Learning Model™**.
2. **Choose one person** who you consider an Independent Learner.
3. **Schedule a meeting with this person.**
4. Use the form below to **plan your conversation** with the employee.

Employee Name: **Program:**

Ideas for Managing Independent Learners	Pre-meeting preparation	Notes
Discuss the learning program. Meet with the team member to discuss what happened during the learning program. Talk about what they learned, and most importantly how their learning links to their current role. Acknowledge completion of the learning and reward their achievement appropriately.	Review the learning program outline. If this is unavailable, find out the content of the program. This is an essential part of preparation.	☐ I have reviewed the program outline.
Agree on learning goals. If they have developed a Skill Development Action Plan discuss the actions that they have listed. Ensure that the actions listed are relevant to their current role. If they have not developed a Skill Development Action Plan, work side-by-side with them to create it. Working together on this will send a strong message of support to the learner.	Print a copy of their job description and keep it on hand ready for the meeting. How does their job role link to the learning that they have just undertaken?	
Monitor their progress towards goal achievement. Ensure that barriers that may get in their way of achieving their learning goals are removed.	What barriers would you predict may get in their way to completing their Skill Development Action Plan? (You'll discover more at the meeting, however some pre-thinking will send a strong message that you are supporting their development)	

ACTIVITY 7: CONTINUED

Ideas for Managing Independent Learners	Pre-meeting preparation	Notes
Stretch learning goals. Where appropriate discuss ways of bringing the employee into the team. Perhaps partner them with an Abandoned or Passive Learner having them provide a 'buddy coaching role'. Alternatively, they could work on developing new workplans, procedures or policies by partnering with a High Performance Learner. This form of co-operative learning may extend the Independent Learner and may encourage their lower performing peers to increase their motivation for learning.	What ideas do you have for them to stretch their goals? (You'll discover more at the meeting, however some pre-thinking will send a strong message that you are supporting their development)	
Discuss Support Mechanisms. Talk about what support is in place for the employee and how they may access the support.	What support mechanisms are already in place?	
	What support mechanisms can you put in place for them?	
	Who else can support them?	
Review Progress and Provide Feedback. Ensure that regular meetings are scheduled to check in on their progress. Continuously provide encouragement.	What is the next step to follow-up progress?	
	When should you schedule the next meeting?	

Now update your Learning Journal (page 87)

MANAGING ABANDONED LEARNERS - ENCOURAGE

The **Abandoned Learner** displays low levels of motivation, and has little support. They require Manager encouragement in order to become a **High Performance Learner.**

They are unlikely to have applied their learning on the job. **In order to encourage an increase in their motivation, first the Manager must display Learning Support for them.**

Ideas for Managing Abandoned Learners

- **Discuss the learning program.** Meet with the team member to discuss what happened during the learning program. Talk about how the learning program links to their current role. Discuss the ways the organization is displaying commitment to the program from their desk, technological support, how you as their manager have supported them or others, and so on.

- **Discover the underlying reasons for not implementing their learning.** Candidly ask why they have not applied what they have learned. Answering this question may be difficult for Abandoned Learners to answer, however in order for them to progress the manager must uncover the reasons why a behavior change has not occurred.

"Learning is like rowing upstream: not to advance is to drop back."

CHINESE PROVERB

- **Agree on learning goals.** If they have developed a Skill Development Action Plan during the program discuss the actions that they have listed. Ensure that the actions listed are relevant to their current role. If they have not developed a Skill Development Action Plan, work side-by-side with them to create it. Working together on this will send a strong message of support to the learner.
- **Gain commitment to progress to action.** Ensure that the employee verbally commits to implementing their Skill Development Action Plan and the timelines associated with it.
- **Monitor their progress** towards goal achievement. Ensure that barriers that may get in their way of achieving their learning goals are removed.
- **Discuss Support Mechanisms.** Talk about what support is in place for them and how they may access the support.
- **Review Progress and Provide Feedback.** Ensure that regular meetings are scheduled to check in on their progress. Continuously provide encouragement.

MANAGING PASSIVE LEARNERS - ENFORCE

The **Passive Learner** displays low levels of motivation despite having organizational and Managerial support. They require counselling in order to become a **High Performance Learner**.

The Passive Learner has been given what is required by way of learning opportunity and support. Quite simply - they are not doing their job. Therefore, this issue is no longer a training issue, but an HR issue focused on their poor performance.

The Manager may counsel the employee using a formal HR process provided by the organization or an informal first-step approach to attempt to change their behavior. Also, the following conversation flow is provided as a first-step guide which aims to encourage employee motivation and create a High Performance Learner.

Ideas for Managing Passive Learners

- **Discuss the learning program.** Meet with the team member to discuss what happened during the learning program. Talk about how the learning program links to their current role. Discuss the ways the organization is displaying commitment to the program – financial investment, people's time away from their desk, technological support, and so on.

- **Discover the underlying reasons for not implementing their learning.** Candidly ask why they have not applied what they have learned. Again, like Abandoned Learners, uncovering the **real** reason for not implementing learning is critical.
- **Agree on learning goals.** If they have developed a Skill Development Action Plan discuss the actions that they have listed. Ensure that the actions listed are relevant to their current role. If they have not developed a Skill Development Action Plan, work side-by-side with them to create it. Working together on this will send a strong message of support to the learner.
- **Gain commitment to progress to action.** Ensure that the employee verbally commits to implementing their Skill Development Action Plan and the timelines associated with it.
- **Monitor their progress** towards goal achievement. Ensure that barriers that may get in their way of achieving their learning goals are removed.
- **Discuss Support Mechanisms.** Talk about what support is in place for them and how they may access the support.
- **Review Progress and Provide Feedback.** Ensure that regular meetings are scheduled to check in on their progress. Continuously provide encouragement.

Complete Activity # 8
Coaching Opportunity - Abandoned and/or Passive Learner

ACTIVITY 8: COACHING OPPORTUNITY - ABANDONED AND / OR PASSIVE LEARNER

1. Review the previous activity where you created your **Team High Performance Learning Model™**.
2. **Choose one person** who you consider an Abandoned or Passive Learner.
3. **Schedule a meeting with this person.**
4. Use the form below to **plan your conversation** with the employee.

Employee Name: **Program:**

Ideas for Managing Abandoned or Passive Learners	Pre-meeting preparation	Notes
Discuss the learning program. Meet with the team member to discuss what happened during the learning program. Talk about how the learning program links to their current role. Discuss the ways the organization is displaying commitment to the program - financial investment, people's time away from their desk, technological support, etc.	Review the learning program outline. If this is unavailable, find out the content of the program.	☐ I have reviewed the program outline.
Discover the underlying reasons for not implementing their learning. Candidly ask why they have not applied what they have learned.	What is the question or questions that you may ask to find out the underlying reasons for them not implementing their learning?	
Agree on learning goals. If they have developed a Skill Development Action Plan discuss the actions that they have listed. Ensure that the actions listed are relevant to their current role. If they have not developed a Skill Development Action Plan, work side-by-side with them to create it. Working together on this will send a strong message of support to the learner.	Print a copy of their job description and keep it on hand ready for the meeting. How does their job role link to the learning that they have just undertaken?	

© 2022, TPC - The Performance Company Pty Limited. All rights reserved.

ACTIVITY 8: CONTINUED

Ideas for Managing Abandoned or Passive Learners	Pre-meeting preparation	Notes
Gain commitment to progress to action. Ensure that the employee verbally commits to implementing their Skill Development Action Plan and the timelines associated with it.	What is the question that you can ask to gain commitment?	
Monitor their progress towards goal achievement. Ensure that barriers that may get in their way of achieving their learning goals are removed.	What barriers would you predict may get in their way to completing their Skill Development Action Plan? (You'll discover more at the meeting, however some pre-thinking will send a strong message that you are supporting their development)	
Discuss Support Mechanisms. Talk about what support is in place for them and how they may access the support.	What support mechanisms are already in place?	
	What support mechanisms can you put in place for them?	
	Who else can support them?	
Review Progress and Provide Feedback. Ensure that regular meetings are scheduled to check in on their progress. Continuously provide encouragement.	What is the next step to follow-up progress?	
	When should you schedule the next meeting?	

Now update your Learning Journal (page 87)

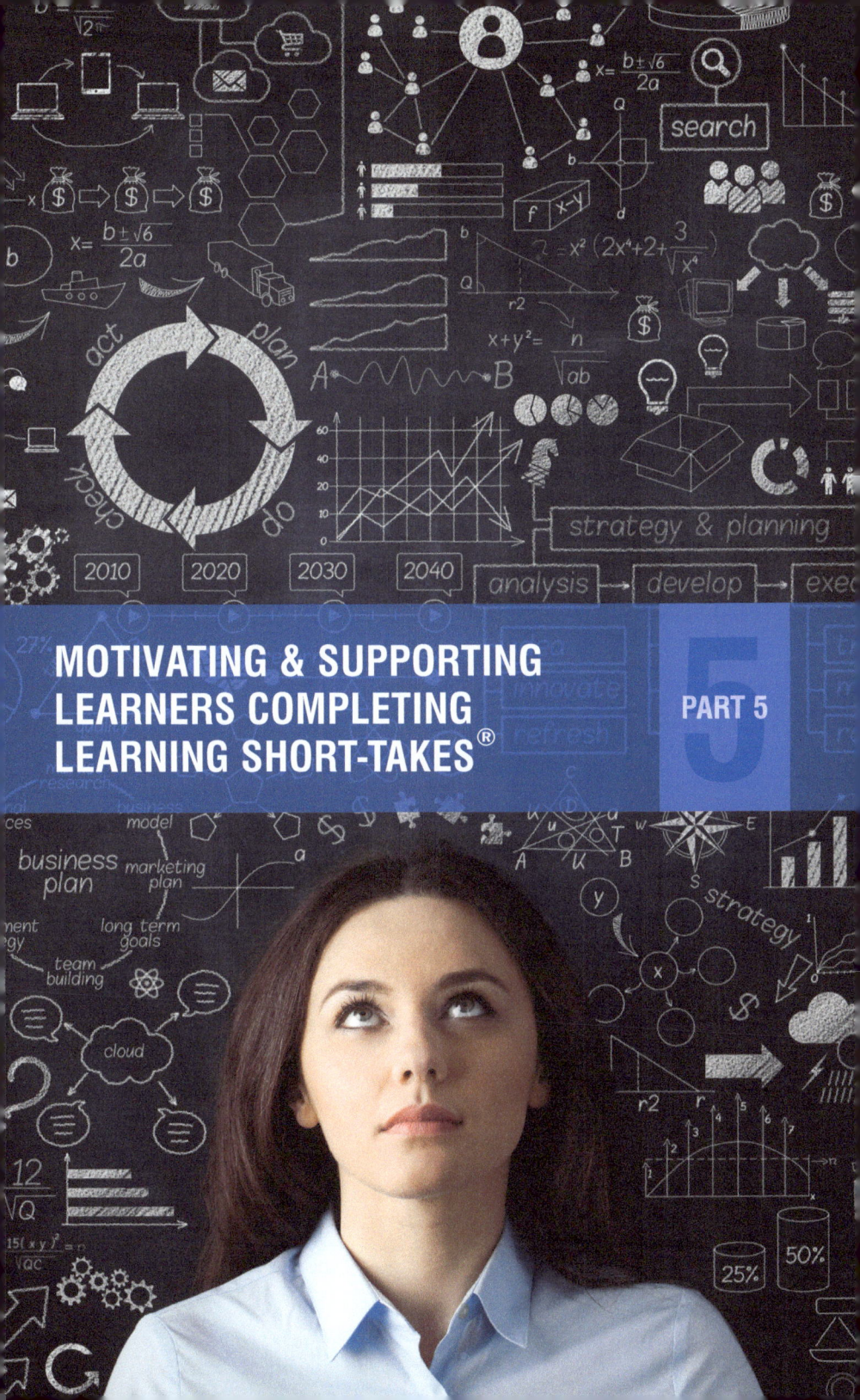

SUPPORTING THE LEARNING SHORT-TAKE® PROCESS

> This section focuses on managing the learning process using Learning Short-takes® however the information is equally applicable to other types of learning programs.

The focus of this section is to provide ideas for Managers to support their team in successfully completing Learning Short-takes®. However, these ideas are very applicable to any type of learning program.

Providing Manager Support - Before, During and After Learning Short-takes®

Managers, supervisors and team leaders can greatly influence the outcomes of training, by providing support for the learning. The goal for the Manager is to create **High Performance Learners.** Before, during and after employees complete the learning program, Managers may be actively involved in the learning process. Manager involvement maximizes application in the workplace of the new skills and knowledge.

18 ideas for Managers to show support for learning

Before the Learning Short-take®

1. Select participants.
2. Review the Learning Short-take® prior to distributing it to employees.
3. Ensure employees understand how to complete the Learning Short-take®.
4. Coach participants on purpose and objectives of the Learning Short-take®.
5. Gain commitment from participants on completing the Learning Short-take®.
6. Plan to apply new skills post- Learning Short-take® with participants.
7. Schedule a meeting for follow-up.

During the Learning Short-take®

8. Protect employees from interruptions during completion of the Learning Short-take®.
9. Ensure participants have at least 90 minutes of time available to assign to completing the Learning Short-take®.
10. Be available to coach participants in Learning Short-take® activities.
11. Encourage participants to become actively involved during the Learning Short-take®.

After the Learning Short-take®

12. Provide practice opportunities immediately after the Learning Short-take®.
13. Discuss participants' Skill Development Action Plan.
14. Lead post-Learning Short-take® debrief sessions with participants and team.
15. Act as a role model to demonstrate desired performance.
16. Monitor participants' application of new skills and give feedback.
17. Ensure further coaching of participants as needed.
18. Remove barriers.

Ideas for Participants to Self-Support the Learning Short-take® Process

Success in Learning Short-takes® is maximized if participants and Managers collaborate in partnership to achieve the learning objectives. While Managers may coach, guide and influence, participants also may be encouraged to take responsibility for their own learning.

High Performance Learners do this with little intervening from Managers, however Managers may influence all participants to share in the responsibility of their learning.

The following table lists ideas that may be discussed by Managers with employees who are about to complete a Learning Short-take®. Also, these ideas may form a checklist for the Manager to check if participants verbal commitment level is aligned to what they are actually doing before, during and after they complete their Learning Short-take®.

"The main difference between high ability achievers and high ability underachievers is that the achievers have learned the attitudes and strategies that enable them to be successful in a learning environment."

JOANNE RAND WHITMORE

13 Ideas for Manager/Employee Learning Discussion

Before the Learning Short-take®

1. Discuss the Learning Short-take® purpose and objectives.
2. Commit to the completion of the Learning Short-take®.

During the Learning Short-take®

3. Ensure that the Learning Short-take® is completed thoroughly and completed in entirety.
4. Participate fully in the Learning Short-take® activities.
5. Create a in-depth Learning Journal.
6. Develop a realistic Skill Development Action Plan.
7. Provide actual work examples for discussion.
8. Identify possible barriers in workplace.

After the Learning Short-take®

9. Debrief Activities, Learning Journal and Skill Development Action Plan and discuss each in detail.
10. Apply new skills promptly.
11. Use job aids and other materials.
12. Collaborate with other participants and facilitators.
13. Request help as required.
13. Discuss how others have implemented their learning and the results that others have had.

Now update your Learning Journal (page 87)

INFLUENCING LEARNER MOTIVATION

The Role of the Manager in providing Motivation to successfully complete Learning Short-takes®

While motivation is an internal driver of behavior, Managers may intentionally positively influence motivation in a learning environment, including completion of Learning Short-takes®, by using the ideas as follows:

- **Establish rapport** with participants and prepare them for learning.
- **Set a tone for completing the Learning Short-take®** - establish a friendly, open atmosphere that shows participants that the Manager is there to help them to learn.
- **Set an appropriate level of difficulty** - high enough to challenge participants but not so high that they become frustrated by information overload.
- **Establish a reward for learning** - demonstrate of the benefits of learning.

3 KEYS TO INFLUENCE LEARNER MOTIVATION

1. In *Reinforcement* of Learned Behaviors - What does success look like?

Positive Reinforcement - reinforces 'good' behavior in the application of new skills.

Negative Reinforcement seeks to eliminate inappropriate behavior in the application of new skills.

- Managers should use both positive and negative reinforcement to help participants keep on track.

2. In ensuring *Retention* - Remember what has been learned

Retention of learning is directly effected by the **amount of practice during the learning.** Ensure that participants complete all Learning Short-take® Activities, update their Learning Journal and create a Skill Development Action Plan.

- **Managers must ensure that participants retain information in order to benefit from the learning.**
- **Managers should emphasize retention and application.** After participants demonstrate correct (desired) performance, they should be urged to practice to maintain desired performance.

"In my experience… achievement depends on willingness to accept a challenge, take risks, make errors and the belief that one has the control over the outcomes. Achievement is hindered by perfectionism, fear of failure, and the belief that control, credit and/or blame belong to someone else."

P. THEROUX

3. In *Transference* of Learning - Apply it on the job

Transfer of learning is the ability to use the information taught in the workplace.

Transference is most likely to occur where the Manager establishes:

- **Content Association** - where participants may associate the new information with something they already know.

- **Content Similarity** - where the information is similar to material that the participant already knows.

- **Critical Attribute Element** - where the information learned is extremely beneficial to the participant's job.

HOW TO INFLUENCE LEARNER MOTIVATION

Respecting Different ways of Learning

Before trying any of the following strategies **it is important to begin by establishing that treating employees differently is not unfair, it is respecting their differences** and treating them the same is not always appropriate or effective.

Ideas for Managers - Learning Short-takes®

Adults learn in different ways. Each of us has a unique combination of learning styles that means that we prefer to learn using different methods.

When adults learn according to their preferred learning style, they learn quicker and retain more. When we learn against our learning style, it's harder to learn and often takes longer.

Motivation plays a huge part in the way participants approach their learning. If the learning program is well written it will take into consideration adult learning styles and be written to meet the needs of all adult learners. When a well written program is combined with high learner motivation, high performance almost naturally occurs.

ADULT LEARNING PRINCIPLES QUICKSTART

There are many different principles and themes about how adults learn. One of the most fundamental is Learning Modalities, including Visual, Auditory and Kinesthetic Learning Styles.

For example, the Learning Short-take® you are completing now meets the 'modalities' of adult learners:

- The Learning Short-take® is printed in color, has many photos, graphics and models, all which assist the *visual learner,* who learns best by seeing the information in color and with pictures.

- For the *auditory learner,* who learn best by hearing (of which there are few adults with this learning style), there are pre-Learning Short-take® discussions with their Manager and post-Learning Short-take® discussions to debrief their work and agree on an action plan. Also, some activities require discussions also heightening the auditory modality.

- The Learning Short-take® also has plenty of activities and a learning journal to complete suiting the *kinesthetic learner,* who learns by doing.

All adult learning programs, should include **at least** these three adult learning styles, catering for all types of adult learners with the aim of maximizing motivation and retention.

10 strategies for Managers to motivate learning

Motivating participants who are completing Learning Short-takes®

There are many strategies for motivating participants in their completion of Learning Short-takes®.

One technique may not be appropriate for all participants at the same time nor effective for even one participant for extended periods of time. Motivational strategies need to be applied individually and changed frequently so that they do not become ineffective through over use.

1. Explain the Learning Short-take® value

The organization must communicate that it feels strongly about the worth of learning.

When Learning Short-takes® are completed by an individual, some visible ways to show the worth of the Learning Short-take® are:

- Ensure that the Learning Short-take® is linked directly to everyday tasks completed by the individual.
- Discuss the learning objectives and why the Learning Short-take® title has been chosen.
- Discuss the advantages of completing the Learning Short-take®.
- Ensure that time is provided in a quiet environment for the employee to complete the Learning Short-take®.

When Learning Short-takes® are completed by each member of a team, some visible ways to show the worth of the Learning Short-take® are:

- Require that the Learning Short-take® is completed by everyone, including the Manager.
- Create a consolidated Skill Development Action Plan, which becomes a Team Action Plan stating what the entire team will do to implement the Learning Short-take®.
- Invite a Senior Leader to attend the Learning Short-take® debrief session, after the Learning Short-take® has been completed to assist with developing the Team Action Plan.
- Reward top employees with additional Learning Short-takes® of their choice that relate to their current or future role.

2. Provide enough time to do the Learning Short-take® properly

Completing Learning Short-takes® in an environment that is rushed or squeezed into other activities is demotivational. Build Learning Short-take® time into peoples' schedules.

3. Distribute Learning Short-takes® to people when they are motivated to learn

This means just-in-time rather than just-in-case training.

4. Zero in on core competencies

Provide Learning Short-takes® that are critical to on-the-job success; avoid information dumping.

5. Allow for expertise sharing

Give team opportunities to share their secrets of success. People like to be recognized for their special skills and knowledge. Peer tutoring and mentoring opportunities motivate learning.

6. Don't overlook adequate practice

It is easy to underestimate proficiency. Asking people to perform a task before they're truly ready is a certain demotivator. Provide encouragement and support during application of new skills.

7. Ensure prompt application of newer skills

The phrase "use it or lose it" sums up the need to implement the new learning immediately rather than at some time in the uncertain future.

8. Encourage Manager support

The Manager is often the key link between what is and is not implemented after completing the Learning Short-take®. The idea is for the Manager to discuss what was learned with the participant upon his / her return to work, how it might be applied in the workplace, and what added support might be needed.

9. Offer Choices

Offering choices develops ownership. When the participant makes decisions, he or she is more likely to accept ownership and control of the results. This sense of control fosters responsibility.

When the control belongs to the Manager so does the ownership. Provide options on which Learning Short-take® titles would best assist participants, or the order in which a series of Learning Short-takes® should be completed.

10. Provide a Secure Environment

Permit participants to fail without penalty. Learning how to deal with failure is critical for developing motivation and successful learning. Participants should learn that they may and must learn from their mistakes.

Fear of failure sometimes causes participants to sabotage their own efforts because deliberate failure is easier to accept than the failures to which they fall victim. No control is equated with being powerless.

Provide support for those undertaking Learning Short-takes®. Changing behavior is difficult for most adult learners and they'll need an opportunity to test drive their skills without fear of failure.

Now update your Learning Journal (page 87)

MANAGING LEARNING SHORT-TAKES® - A STEP-BY-STEP GUIDE

PART 6

MANAGERS GUIDE - BEFORE THE LEARNING SHORT-TAKE®

This section focuses on managing the learning process using Learning Short-takes® however the information is equally applicable to other types of learning programs.

Following is a three-step process for successfully starting the Learning Short-take® Process

- **Step 1 - Introducing the Learning Short-take®**
- **Step 2 - Communicating the Learning Short-take® Objectives**
- **Step 3 - Gaining Commitment**

Step 1 - Introducing the Learning Short-take®

When an employee or team is assigned a Learning Short-take® to complete it's imperative that the Manager partners with them to support the learning process. TPC refers to this as Partnership Learning where the employee is supported by the Manager and in turn will encourage anticipation, participation, and a high level of motivation to complete and apply their learning.

This support demonstrates to employees the importance of the learning and why the organization has invested in the Learning Short-takes®.

Sample: Manager Starting the Conversation…with One Person

> "As we discussed in your performance review, one of your goals is to manage the incoming customer inquiries. I know that you are concerned about adding this task to your very busy day and we talked about adding some more techniques on prioritizing, goal setting and managing your time. It's important to me that you feel supported with this new task. I have a Learning Short-take® here for you - Effective Time Management.
>
> The aim of this Learning Short-take® is to develop your skills in those areas, and because you don't have to go to a formal training course, this is something that you may complete during your work day. I'd like to spend a few minutes with you now so that you are confident to complete the Learning Short-take®…"

Sample: Manager Starting the Conversation…with a Team

" *In the last few meetings we've been talking about the commencement of new tasks and responsibilities to our team. Over the next few weeks, we'll have taken over responsibility for processing all incoming customer inquiries, handling customer issues that have been mailed to us, and responding to customer complaints. With that in mind, we all need to sharpen our skills in how we manage our time, especially in the areas of prioritizing daily tasks, working towards our individual and team goals and making sure that we maintain a healthy outlook to work. This Learning Short-take® is Effective Time Management and I thought as a team we could all benefit from completing it – me included! The aim of this Learning Short-take® is to develop our skills in these areas. It will only take about 90 minutes to complete and may be completed during work time. When we meet again as a team in two weeks from now, please ensure that you've completed it. I'd like to spend a few minutes with you now so that you are confident to complete the Learning Short-take®…* "

Step 2 - Communicating the Learning Short-take® Objectives

Managers should communicate the objectives and goal of the Learning Short-take® to the employee. **It's important for the employee to have a solid understanding of why they are being asked to complete the Learning Short-take® and how it will benefit them.**

Questions for Managers to ask when distributing the Learning Short-take®

- What are your most pressing problems?
- What are your interests in this topic?
- What do you hope to get out of this Learning Short-take®?
- What would the value be to you from this Learning Short-take®?

The answers to these types of questions are likely to provide insight into learner motivation, as well as desirable behavioral outcomes.

Sample: Manager Continuing the Conversation...with One Person or a Team

" ... I'd like to spend a few minutes with you now so that you are confident to complete the Learning Short-take®. Let's open the Learning Short-take®, you'll see all of the instructions to complete it are outlined. You'll notice that you have a Participant Guide, some Activities, a Learning Journal and Skill Development Action Plan. Completing the Learning Short-take® is straightforward.

To begin, I'd like to go focus on the Learning Objectives for this Learning Short-take®. [Turn to Learning Objectives page. Go through each objective linking where appropriate to the individuals/team role.]

Follow the Participant Guide, and when instructed, go to the relevant activity and complete it. When asked, update your Learning Journal. A Learning Journal is a summary of what you've learnt and what you'll put into action. It's a great way of making sure you are capturing all of your key learnings.

At the end, you'll complete your Skill Development Action Plan. That will be your list of actions that you'll take and how you'll implement what you've learnt on the job.

So, from what I've described, what do you see as the value from completing this Learning Short-take® for you? [Conversation continues]

So that we can kick start the learning process, let's make a list of what you'd like to achieve from this Learning Short-take®. [Conversation continues]

What questions do you have about completing the Learning Short-take®?... "

Step 3 - Gaining Commitment

Employees are more likely to complete their Learning Short-take® if they have verbally committed to doing so. In his book, Influence, Robert Cialdini discusses the naturally occurring influence pattern of 'commitment and consistency', that is, people are more likely to be consistent with their promise if they've verbally committed to it in front of others.

Finishing the conversation... with one person or a team

" What questions do you have about completing the Learning Short-take®? [Answer questions]. Let's set a date now that we may meet again to discuss your Learning Short-take®. [Set a mutually convenient meeting time for approximately 30 minutes.]

At that meeting, we'll review each of the activities, and discuss in detail your Learning Journal and Skill Development Action Plan. It's important that you bring your Learning Short-take® to the meeting.

Are you clear that you need to complete all of the activities, Learning Journal and create your Skill Development Action Plan? [Get commitment from employee.]

Do I have your assurance that you'll complete everything by [meeting date]? [Gain verbal commitment from employee.]

If you need any help at all, please feel welcome to ask for my assistance. I'm really looking forward to discussing your finished Learning Short-take® with you at our meeting. "

Now update your Learning Journal (page 87)

**Analyze the following tool.
Think about how you may use this tool.**

PRE-LEARNING SHORT-TAKE® MANAGER CONVERSATION TOOL

FREE DOWNLOAD

To download this tool go to https://www.catherinemattiske.com/books and follow the online instructions.

MANAGERS GUIDE - AFTER THE LEARNING SHORT-TAKE®

Debriefing the Learning Short-take®

After an employee finishes the Learning Short-take®, the Manager should have a meeting with them to debrief the results and discuss the Skill Development Action Plan. In particular the Manager should focus on:

1. Checking the results of the activities
2. Reviewing the Learning Journal
3. Discussing in detail the Skill Development Action Plan

The following step-by-step guide may assist in the flow of the debrief conversation. The steps are:

- **Step 1 - General information about completion of the Learning Short-take®**
- **Step 2 - Discuss appropriateness of the Learning Short-take® title**
- **Step 3 - Check the learning and Skill Development Action Plan**
- **Step 4 - What else?**

The following questions are listed as a guide for Managers to ask employees at the debrief meeting. These questions may be used effectively for both individuals and groups who have completed a single Learning Short-take® title, or a series of Learning Short-take® titles.

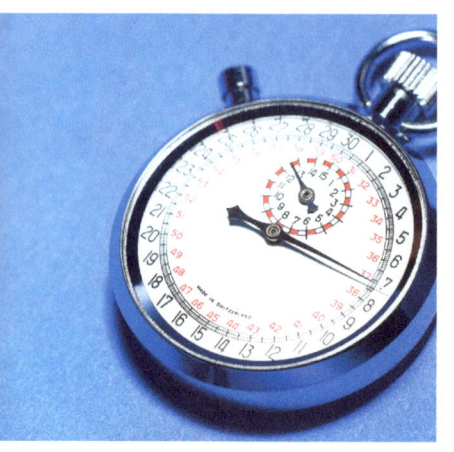

Step 1 – General information about completion of the Learning Short-take®

- When did you finish the Learning Short-take®?
    - Managers Guide - the answer to this question may assist you later in the conversation. You'll expect good recall of material if the participant has just completed their Learning Short-take®.

- How long did it take you to complete the Learning Short-take®?
    - Managers Guide – Learning Short-takes® are designed to take approximately 90 minutes to complete.

    If an employee takes less time than 90 minutes, talk about specific parts of the Learning Short-take® to ensure it was completed in full. Review activities and discuss their answers.

    Taking longer than 90 minutes is often a positive thing! High Performance Learners often take more than 90 minute to complete the Learning Short-take. They may do additional research into the topic using the internet, or may begin transferring their learning to their workplace projects.

    However, if employees are not High Performance Learners and have taken an excessive time to complete the Learning Short-take® they may have struggled with the level of content of the Learning Short-take®. Ensure that you coach them to a successful outcome by reviewing the material and if necessary, working with them side-by-side to complete the activities and link the outcome to their role.

Step 2 - Discuss appropriateness of the Learning Short-take® title

- Was the level of the content appropriate for you? Did you have difficulty with any of the activities? What did you find straightforward? What did you find interesting?
- How is the Learning Short-take® content relevant to your role?
- How is the Learning Short-take® appropriate for the projects you have now? Which projects in particular do you consider this information useful for?

Step 3 - Check the Learning Journal and Skill Development Action Plan

- What one 'big thing' did you learn from completing the Learning Short-take®?
    - Managers Guide - participants should be able to remember their key learning without checking back to the Learning Short-take®. If they are having difficulty remembering, use the Learning Journal as a prompt.
- Would you walk through each of the Activities with me and we can discuss your answers to the activities?
    - Managers Guide – review each Activity. Discuss case studies with them and try to link the case study or activity to their current job role. A question such as "how does this relate to your job?" is an appropriate open question to encourage conversation.

- May I review your Learning Journal? What have been your key learnings from completing this Learning Short-take®?
    - Managers Guide - review their Learning Journal. Participants are asked to complete their Learning Journal, noting key learnings and things to remember, at various intervals throughout the Learning Short-take®. The Learning Journal is the basis of the Skill Development Action Plan.
- May I discuss your Skill Development Action Plan? What are your actions? Are they realistic? Do you have a timeline for each Action Item?
    - Managers Guide - review their Skill Development Action Plan. Participants are asked to complete their Skill Development Action Plan using the Learning Journal and relevant Activities as a basis for planning how they may implement their learning. Ensure that the actions are relevant, specific, and have deadlines for completion.
- What will you achieve in the next 30 days?
- May I document your actions that you are committing to?
    - Managers Guide - use the following Post-Learning Short-take® Conversation Tool to assist you with the conversation from herein.
- How will you measure your success from your Actions? Who will give you that feedback?
- How can I support you in completing your Skill Development Action Plan?

Step 4 – What else?

- What questions you have about the Learning Short-take®?
- Who else in our team would you recommend complete the Learning Short-take®?
- Do I have your commitment that you'll now implement your Skill Development Action Plan?
    - Managers Guide - asking for commitment is an important step. People are more likely to be consistent with implementing their Skill Development Action Plan if they have verbally given their Manager their commitment.

Now update your Learning Journal (page 87)

**Analyze the following tool.
Think about how you may use this tool.**

POST-LEARNING SHORT-TAKE® MANAGER CONVERSATION TOOL

FREE DOWNLOAD

To download this tool go to **https://www.catherinemattiske.com/** books and follow the online instructions.

Section 2
LEARNING JOURNAL

The Learning Journal is used throughout the process to record your key learnings, hot tips and things to remember.

Update your Learning Journal at anytime. Ensure you complete your Learning Journal after you finish each activity. Then turn back to the Learning Short-take® to continue your learning.

LEARNING JOURNAL

As you work through this Learning Short-take®, make detailed notes on this page of the lessons you have learned and any useful skill areas. For each lesson or refresher point think about how you could further develop this skill. Your coach will want to discuss these with you in your Skill Development Action Planning meeting.

*"…that is what learning is.
You suddenly understand something you've understood all your life, but in a new way."*

DORIS LESSING

"Anyone who stops learning is old, whether at twenty or eighty."

HENRY FORD

"The wise do at once what the fool does later."
BALTASAR GRACIAN (1601-58), SPANISH JESUIT PRIEST AND AUTHOR.

Learning or Idea	Action to be taken	Result Expected

Learning Journal - continued

Learning or Idea	Action to be taken	Result Expected

> *"Anyone who stops learning is old, whether at twenty or eighty."*
> HENRY FORD

Learning or Idea	Action to be taken	Result Expected

"

"There is a difference between wishing for something and being ready to receive it. No one is ready for a thing unless he believes he can acquire it."

NAPOLEON HILL

"

Section 3

SKILL DEVELOPMENT ACTION PLAN

Your Skill Development Action Plan is the last Step in the process. After you have completed the Learning Short-take® and all Activities, update your Learning Journal, then complete this section.

SKILL DEVELOPMENT ACTION PLAN

This is the most important part of the program - your individual Skill Development Action Plan.

You need to complete this plan before meeting with your manager or prior to on-going coaching. You will discuss it in detail with your manager or coach as he or she will ensure that you have everything you need to complete the tasks and activities.

Once you have completed your **Skill Development Action Plan** schedule a meeting time with your manager or coach to review your plan. Take your Learning Short-take® and all other documentation received during the training course to this meeting.

Remember - you have committed to your **Skill Development Action Plan**, and need to make time to complete your tasks!

"The mind, once stretched by a new idea, never regains its original dimensions."

OLIVER WENDELL HOLMES

"Whatever you can do or dream you can - begin it. Boldness has genius, power and magic."

JOHANN WOLFGANG VON GOETHE

"Imagination is the eye of the soul."
JOSEPH JOUBERT (1754-1824)

Task or activity (Be specific)	Measure (this will help you to know you have achieved it)	Date (Be specific)
Reflect on your Learning Journal. Transfer action items that you can apply to your job. Ensure that you include some 'stretch goals' and also a blend of short, medium and long term goals.	Apart from you, who else is needed to assist you in achieving your goal.	Be specific. A general date such as 'Quarter 1', 'August', or 'by end of year' is vague and more likely to result in not achieving your target. Be specific – e.g. 22nd November.

IDEAS FOR DISCUSSION WITH MY MANAGER

Ideas

CONGRATULATIONS!

You've now completed this Learning Short-take®.

Meet with your Manager/Coach to discuss your
Skill Development Action Plan.

> *"Do what you fear most and you control fear."*
>
> TOM HOPKINS

QUICK REFERENCE

This Quick Reference provides you with a summary of key concepts, models and reference material from Learning Short-takes®. We have also included some quotations to ponder.

Use this section as a quick reference to keep your learning active.

Quick Reference

> **When the student is ready, the master appears.**
>
> Buddhist Proverb

Partnership Learning means that the Manager partners with the employee before, during and after the learning to maximize the change of behavior.

Quick Reference

No Change of Behavior

=

No Training has Occurred

Mattiske's High Performance Learning Model™

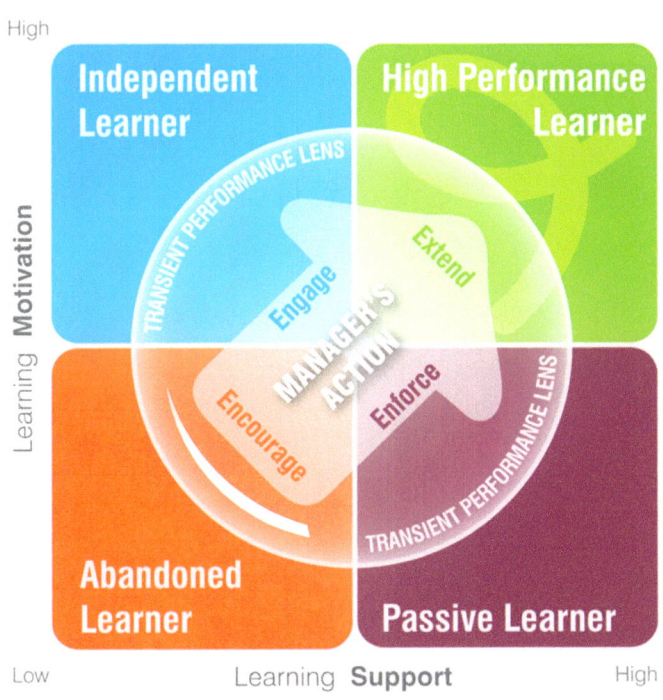

Quick Reference

The Transient Learner

One person may transition from one Learner Type to another depending on the learning that they are about to encounter. They may even transition during a training program, entering the training program as one Learner Type and then changing midstream (positively or negatively) as another Learner Type.

Learner Type:
The High Performance Learner

High Motivation (Internal) + High Support (External)

Before the Learning

- Completed pre-requisites
- Know training location and times
- Made personal arrangements
- Begun learning process prior to class
- Briefed by Manager on expectations
- Know how the learning fits to their current or future role

Quick Reference

Learner Type:
The High Performance Learner

During the Learning

- Active learner
- Asks questions
- Takes notes
- Learning is their focus - not easily distracted
- Doesn't get stuck - either asks a question or 'parks' the query for another time and moves ahead with their learning
- Thinking of ways to apply their learner
- 'Can't wait to get back to work and apply it' attitude

Learner Type:
The High Performance Learner

After the Learning

- Quick to implement learning
- Proactively reports progress to Manager
- Shows Manager how they will apply their learning (not just what they've learned)
- Informal learning continues through self discovery
- Will teach others

Quick Reference

Learner Type: The Independent Learner

High Motivation (Internal) + Low Support (External)

Spotting the Independent Learner

- Proactively provides well-researched personal learning plan
- Individual Development Plans well documented at Performance Review Meetings
- Works on external training programs during work time
- Learning is about them, not how their learning will help the organization
- No proactive reporting back to Manager on progress

Learner Type: The Abandoned Learner

Low Motivation (Internal) + Low Support (External)

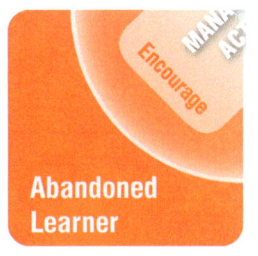

The Abandoned Learner's manager and organization is doing little to provide support and encouragement for their learning further supporting their lack of motivation.

Quick Reference

Learner Type: The Passive Learner

Low Motivation (Internal) + High Support (External)

The Passive Learner has a variety of formal and non-formal support mechanisms in place, has attended the learning program, yet still hasn't implemented what has been learned and has NOT changed their behavior.

Maximizing High Performance Learners: EXTEND

Goal: Extend them to achieve even higher levels of performance

Ideas for Coaching High Performance Learners

- Reward High Performance Learners on their achievement
- Agree on Learning Goals
- Monitor their Progress
- Stretch Learning Goals
- Discuss Support Mechanisms
- Review Progress and Provide Feedback

Quick Reference

Maximizing Independent Learners: ENGAGE

Goal: Engage and coach them to share their learning and be part of the team to achieve high levels of performance

Ideas for Coaching Independent Learners

- Discuss the Learning Program
- Agree on Learning Goals
- Monitor their Progress
- Stretch Learning Goals
- Discuss Support Mechanisms
- Review Progress and Provide Feedback

Maximizing Passive Learners: ENCOURAGE

Goal: Coach them to increase their motivation by first providing learning support.

Ideas for Coaching Passive Learners

- Discuss the Learning Program
- Discover the underlying reasons for not implementing their learning
- Agree on Learning Goals
- Gain Commitment to progress to Action
- Monitor their Progress
- Discuss Support Mechanisms
- Review Progress and Provide Feedback

Quick Reference

Maximizing Abandoned Learners: ENFORCE

Goal: Counsel using informal or formal processes to enforce to them that the learning is an expectation within their current role.

Ideas for Coaching Abandoned Learners

- Discuss the Learning Program
- Discover the underlying reasons for not implementing their learning
- Agree on Learning Goals
- Gain Commitment to progress to Action
- Monitor their Progress
- Discuss Support Mechanisms
- Review Progress and Provide Feedback

Ways for Managers to show Learning Support

- Ensure participants are confident BEFORE THE LEARNING, know what's expected, and what the learning entails

- Protect participants DURING THE LEARNING and participate in the learning with them where appropriate

- AFTER THE LEARNING provide opportunities to implement learning, discuss Skill Development Action Plans, act as a Role Model and provide coaching and feedback.

Quick Reference

Ways for Managers to Influence Learner Motivation

- Know what success looks like, and REINFORCE good behavior during feedback and coaching

- Ensure participants RETAIN information via review of activities, action plans, learning journals that were completed in class, and the on-going use of job aids, notes and handouts.

- Ensure participants TRANSFER learning and apply it on the job.

10 more Strategies for Motivating Learning for Learning Short-takes®

1. Explain the Learning Value
2. Provide enough time to do the Learning Short-take® properly
3. Distribute Learning Short-takes® to people when they are motivated to learn
4. Zero in on core competencies
5. Allow for expertise sharing
6. Don't overlook adequate practice
7. Ensure prompt application of newer skills
8. Encourage Manager support
9. Offer choices
10. Provide a Secure Environment

Quick Reference

Adult Learning Principles Quickstart

Learning Modalities

"What do they see"
Visual Learner

"What do they hear"
Auditory Learner

"What do they do"
Kinesthetic Learner

Managers Guide - Before and After the Learning Short-take™

Before the Learning Short-take®
- Introduce the Learning Short-take®
- Communicate the Learning Short-take® Objective
- Gain Commitment

Use the Pre-Learning Short-take® Manager Conversation Tool

After the Learning Short-take®
- Get information about how the Learning Short-take® was completed
- Discuss appropriateness of the Learning Short-take®
- Check the learning & Skill Development Action Plan
- Discuss next steps - What else?

Use the Post-Learning Short-take® Manager Conversation Tool

Quick Reference

Pre-Learning Short-take® Manager Conversation Tool

Go to **https://www.catherinemattiske.com/books** to download this tool

Post-Learning Short-take® Manager Conversation Tool

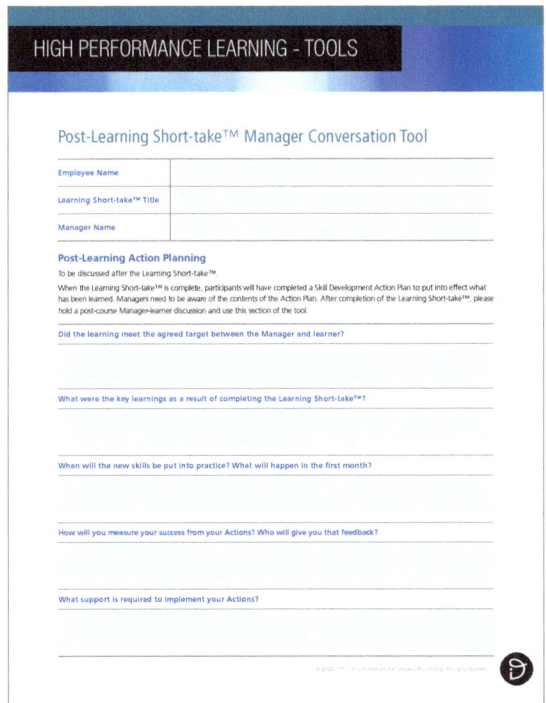

Go to **https://www.catherinemattiske.com/books** to download this tool

"
"In real life the greatest heroes are often found among the most ordinary people.

Do not wait for extraordinary circumstances to do good; try to use ordinary situations."

JEAN PAUL RICHTER

NEXT STEPS

Congratulations! You have now completed this Learning Short-take® title. The entire list of Learning Short-takes® can be found on the catherinemattiske.com website.

In this section we have suggested Learning Short-take® titles for you that will build your learning. You may order these Learning Short-takes® online at https://www.catherinemattiske.com/books or from your bookstores.

Adult Learning Principles 1
Understanding the Ways Adults Learn

Learning Short-take® Outline

Adult Learning Principles 1 combines self-study with realistic workplace activities for trainers, educators, facilitators and managers to develop skills and knowledge in the principles of adult learning. It will add adult learning techniques to your 'grab bag' of learning design tools for improved learning outcomes. After evaluation of your current approach to learning design, you will learn to develop new and innovative strategies to engage learners at every level. Significantly increasing participant retention and training results **Adult Learning Principles 1** will fuel your confidence in designing successful training workshops and e-Learning every time.

The principles of adult learning work on the basis that we all learn differently, and the way we like to receive and interpret information varies from person to person. Trainers and facilitators who use a combination of adult learning principles to provide balance in their programs increase the chances of keeping all participants focused and engaged throughout the learning process. **Adult Learning Principles 1** will assist you in building a good mix of adult learning styles which is critical in ensuring learning, thorough participant retention and workplace application.

Adult Learning Principles 1 includes the job aid **Strategies for Meeting Global and Specific Needs**, the **Adult Learning Principles Quick Reference Wall Chart and the Activity Booklet**, provided as free downloadable tools.

Course Content

- Part 1: Understanding Adult Learners
- Part 2: Adult Learning Principle 1 - Global vs Specific Learners
- Part 3: Adult Learning Principle 2 - Learning Style - Modalities
- Part 4: Adult Learning Principle 3 - Learning Types - The 4Mat System

Learning Objectives

- Successfully match adult learning terms with definitions.
- Determine your personal Learning Style preference.
- List and give working examples of three Adult Learning Principles – Global vs Specific, Learning Styles and Learning Types.
- Develop strategies and ideas to link Adult Learning Principles with Instructional Design.

Adult Learning Principles 2
Blending Interaction with Measurement

Course Content

- Part 1: Fundamentals of Effective Learning
- Part 2: Measurement Myths
- Part 3: Measuring Through Interaction & Review
- Part 4: Learning Activities
- Part 5: Review Activities
- Part 6: Bringing It All Together

Learning Short-take® Outline

Adult Learning Principles 2 combines self-study with realistic workplace activities to develop skills in learning interaction and measurement. Building on Adult Learning Principles 1, this Learning Short-take® examines the importance of demonstrating the impact of learning. It explores common myths of learning measurement and using interaction to support and measure learning. For learning designers, trainers, educators, facilitators, and managers the library of training activities provided allow you to develop new and innovative strategies to assess learning during workshops, courses, sessions, and eLearning modules.

In the corporate world, measuring and demonstrating the value of learning is discussed frequently. Organizations are searching for the perfect way to link human resource capability and learning outcomes with business strategy. To achieve this result, it is important to know how to effectively deploy and measure learning. During the learning itself we have the greatest opportunity to observe learning transfer taking place.

Adult Learning Principles 2 provides practical know-how and a library of activities that can be used to measure learning during any learning experience. It features **Mattiske's Training Focus Model** and includes the **Training Review Analysis Tool** as a free download.

Learning Objectives

- Know the underlying drivers of successful learning outcomes
- Identify common myths about measuring learning
- Recognize the value of Interaction and Review for better learning measurement
- Define the levels of participant interaction and adopt a mindset for interaction in learning
- List the different types of learning activities
- Identify and explain the different types of Review
- Collect a bank of practical learning and review activities
- Create a Skill Development Action Plan

Debrief and Feedback Strategies
A Trainer's Toolkit for Maximizing Learning Activities

Learning Short-take® Outline

Debrief and Feedback Strategies combines self-study with real workplace activities to develop skills in delivering training feedback and debriefing learning activities.

Debrief and Feedback Strategies will guide you in evaluating your current approaches to delivering feedback and activity debriefs, and in developing new and innovative approaches to maximize learning for instructor-led, eLearning and other types of training.

Participants in training value constructive feedback over tangible rewards. The effective use of providing feedback and debriefing activities is vital for transfer of learning, participant motivation and workplace application. Learning and application opportunities can be wasted when participants fail to receive relevant information about their performance. By providing you with a better understanding of useful debriefing and feedback delivery, **Debrief and Feedback Strategies** will help you capitalize on your training sessions.

Debrief and Feedback Strategies includes the **Higher-Order Question Job Aid**, provided as a free downloadable tool.

Course Content

- Part 1: Feedback
- Part 2: Debrief

Learning Objectives

- Explain the value of feedback in training and workplace performance improvement
- Use appropriate techniques for delivering feedback
- Select and apply effective e-learning feedback strategies
- Design training and other types of workplace debriefs
- Explain and list debrief questioning techniques
- Create a Skill Development Action Plan

www.catherinemattiske.com